Behold, the Garden

Greg Delanty

&

Young Writers Project

Fomite
Burlington, VT

ISBN-13: 978-1-967022-06-9
Library of Congress Control Number: 2025937867

Fomite
58 Peru Street
Burlington, VT 05401
www.fomitepress.com

04/11/2026
#616161

Contents

Interlude

A New Field Guide to People (continued)

Envoy

Behold the Garden is set in Dante type (which originated in the 14th century with Giovanni Boccaccio's "Treatise in Praise of Dante"). Delanty's own sonnets are in terza rima (first twelve lines), invented by Dante."

Preface

Behold, the Garden was originally intended to be a book containing only my own poems, and it was put together after the publication of my poetry collection, *No More Time*. This book is a twin sibling of *No More Time*, though more a fraternal twin — "dizygotic" — than an identical twin. Both books are about the environment, climate change, and the general state of our planet, and they are approached in a similar fashion. *No More Time* was published in 2020, but nearly all of the poems in that earlier book and this book were written between 2015 and 2017. Putting more poems on this subject and form into *No More Time* would have overwhelmed it — although I regret not having put in "Virus", which unwittingly presaged Covid. Some of my poems here in *Behold the Garden* may be overly didactic, evidence, perhaps, that language itself cannot contain what humans have brought about — a good excuse for bad poems, but also an authentic artistic reason for unsuccessful poems, arch as that sounds. Who knows, but this collection, snubbing tergiverse, might still manage to lift above its weight like the ant of the sonnet *'Formicidae'*.

I held back publishing *Behold the Garden* for the reason above, but also because it seemed too close to the book *No More Time*. It needed another dimension to renew it, to make it worthwhile. For a number of years now I have been reading the work, mostly poems, of Young Writers Project, which appeared weekly in the 'Hometown' section of the *Burlington Free Press*. It highlighted writing, photos, and art submitted to the YWP's website by youths between eight and eighteen years of age. I was often surprised and delighted by how affective these poems were/are. I would cut poems from the newspaper that struck me. I even purchased all the anthologies that were published each year right up to 2023 and read everything from start to finish. I had the notion of asking Young Writers Project if I could select work for an anthology of the YWP going back to when it began in 2006 — I still hope that this anthology will be published.

While putting together *Behold, the Garden*, it struck me that I should include the work of young poets and writers, and I proceeded to match the work of the YWP with my own poems. So here is the result. I did not choose the work of the young writers solely on aesthetic merit, but on the authenticity of their feelings. Their work should not be consigned and confined totally to the modern paradigms of poetry and art. As I said about my own poems here, language itself cannot contain what humans have brought about. This book, the young people's writing and my own, should also be viewed as a whole, a kind of spirit biosphere of our times.

Nine of my poems were published as a special edition titled *The Atlas Trap*, handset in 2022 by Paulette Myers, with accompanying art work by Zachery Skinner in the 'Trafficking in Poetry' series. The poem 'Formicidae' was published in the PoemCity 2022 series, Montpelier. The poems 'Orca', 'Parrot' and 'Lonesome George' were first published in *Agenda*. A number of other poems from this book were first published in the online magazines of Green Mountain Review and Green Writers Press, and in print in *Southward*. I would like to thank the editors. A version of the poem "The Noble Lie" was first published in *The New Citizen Army* by Combat Paper Press as "Where the Truth Lies", using handmade paper made from the pulped uniforms of those who survived conflict and military service.

All proceeds of this book, once it has covered its own expense, will go to 350.org, 350vermont.org and The Chernobyl Children's Project.

Greg Delanty,
Burlington Vermont, September 1st, 2025

Dedication

This book is for everyone, of course, but it is also especially dedicated to the younger people of today, a small number of family and friends' children I name here: Leo Aloisi, Miro Aloisi, Travis Arney, Patrick Arney, Annabelle Arney, Caroline Arney, Colton Arney, Barrett Arney, McKelvey Catherine Ayres, Virginia Margaret Ayres, Samuel Dylan Barber, Elijah Baraw, Henry Baraw, Dylan Berry, Oscar Bolger, Donnacha Bolger, Diarmuid Bolger Mark Bosiuk, Mia Dorothy Bray-McKenna, Leander Buckley, William Burnett, Hannah Carson, Frankie Carson, Shay-Iarla Condon, Noah Cotter, Tom Cotter, Sibéal Cuffe and Cian Cuffe, Oran Brennan Dailly, Diarmuid James Deady, Oisín James Deady, Daniel Delanty, Niamh Delanty, Saorlaith Delanty, Bláthnaid Desmond, Clodagh Faye Desmond, Conal Desmond, Conal Óg Desmond, Donnchadh Desmond, Fiadh Desmond, Hugo Kai Desmond, Leon Demsmond, Pádraig Desmond, Alexander Ivan Dykstra Collier, Maximilian James Dykstra Collier, John Cunningham, Daniel Fagan, Ellie Farr, Eneko Farr, Phoebe Kathleen Gardiner, Olivia Clare Gardiner, Declan Gilman, Emerson Gilman, McCoy Gilman, Ana Sofía Gilman-Urbina, Lorenzo Gilman-Urbina, Madeleine Greaves, Gina Hanrahan, Isabelle Hanrahan, Kathryn H. Henry, Thomas P Henry, James Romare Jackson, Finn-Riordan Jones, Sadhbh Kelleher, Andi Kelleher, Ellen Ruth Kujawa, Laura Elizabeth Kujawa, Ana Kusserow-Lair, Willem Kusserow-Lair, Katherine Laird, Harvey Laird, Connor Leavy Murphy, Niamh Leavy Murph , Yvie MacDonald-Dowd, Zazie MacDonald-Dowd, Ziggy MacDonald-Dowd, Anna O'Mahony, Patrick O'Mahony, Heather McCabe, Ethan McCabe, Lauren McCabe, Aurelia Mathúna-McDonald, Isabella McCann, John Michael McCann, Christian McCann, Éabha McCarthy, Langston McCullogh, Archie McDonnell, Louie McDonnell, Anakin Mellet, Saskia Mellet,

Ruscha Merilion, Sacha Merilion, Siobhán Ní Dhuinnín, Cáit Ní Dhuinnín, Martin O'Brien, Naoise O'Brien, Stephen O'Brien, Seán Ó Duinnín, Daniel O'Hanrahan, Sadhbh O'Hanrahan, Matilda O'Keeffe, Rory O'Keeffe, Aurelia Mahoney, Aye Mahoney, Fionn Mahoney, Riain Mahoney, Sally Mahoney, Áine Ní Mhuirthile, Cian Ó Muirthile, Eoin Ó Muirthile, Oisín Ó Muirthile, Oran Ó Muirthile, Ruán Ó Muirthile, Eleanor Oser, Briana Oser, Damian Patrin, Nate Patrin, Kieran O'Shea, Ida Parini, Massimo Parini, Everett Parini, Sylvia Parini, Arthur Preston-Matto, Coulson Preston-Matto, Sophie Xiaozhen Pollak, Anna Riley-Shepard, Claire Robinson, Isaac Robinson, Owen Robinson, Samuel Robinson, Madeleine Rowley, Hazel Saunders, Willa Saunders, Dominic Sheehey, Caroline Sheehey, Beckett Simon, Eliza Simon, Beatrice Stoica, Ariadne Stoica, Rachel Smith, Chesley Smith, Malcolm Solomon, Winslow Solomon, Frank Riordan-Jones, Greta Thunberg, Issa Van Criekinge, Gavin Wall-Jones, Juliette Wall-Jones, Ben Aaron Webster, Susan Webster, Shaman Webster, Christian Webster, Charlie Anne Webster, Eli Webster, Logan Webster, Anastasia White, Kieran Williams, Ruby Williams, Bram Williams, Louis Williams, Heather Wry, Katie Wry, Erin Wry, Freya Wyley-Sirr, and all future generations. We want you to know, and not just for ourselves, that some of the people gone before you are trying not to let you down.

I also would like to thank the following people: Donna Bister, John Bourke, David Cavanagh, Dan Johnson, Patricia McCarthy, Marcus Frederick and the magazine *Agenda*, Lee Oser, Adi Roche and the Chernobyl Children's Project, and 350.org.

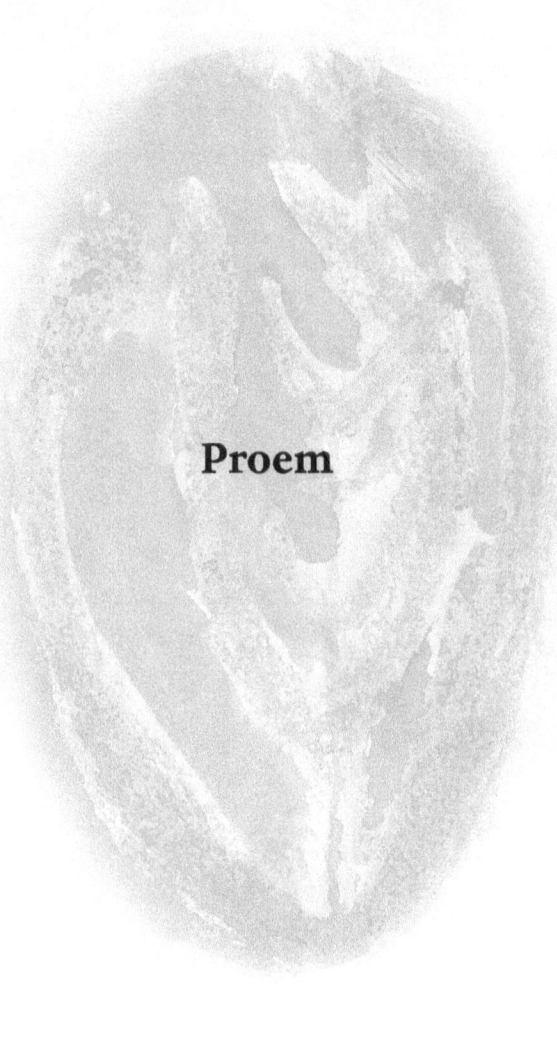

Proem

The First Story

The email — telling a friend *we're not too bad considering*
        the state of the world — crosses the Atlantic
with the touch of a key. The leaves of an evergreen blow
        like a shoal of jade fish returning to the same place.
A cardinal in his scarlet robes pecks the feeder.
        The bells of the Angelus ring from St Joseph's,
the Angel of the Lord declares unto Mary. The infant
        of my childhood is back on Earth again, the God
I've ceased to believe in, the lifebelt that keeps believers afloat
        in the storm of being here, issuing tickets
to the hereafter ever since that episode in the garden,
        the tall tale of our banishment concocted by some storyteller
who'd be so flummoxed we've taken it for gospel
        he'd simply say: "Look around you now. Behold, the garden."

                    from *The Greek Anthology, Book XVII*
                    (retitled *Book Seventeen* in the US Edition)

Bluebird Song

Narges Anzali, 16, Weybridge, VT

I.
I wish I hadn't been born in the Age of
Extinction.
I really don't think my origami heart was
made for this,
this list of things that disappeared into
the folds long before I was 3, 4, 5.
How many last ones am I throwing in
the trash?
How many last ones am I scraping on
my tongue?
Where are the last papyrus makers
in Egypt?
Where are the last speakers of my
tongue?

II.
You didn't know the spirits talk to me,
but they do. You don't know that there is
a ghost following me,
but there is. You ask me to define
immigrant for a prompt in our English class
and I say someone who doesn't need an
English class. You ask me
to define broken in our English class and
I say my butchered mother tongue.
Then we go read an article about a
species we will never see,
a type of bluebird that I can't remember

the Latin name of,
and that seems important because if I
don't remember the bluebird,
then who does? If the Library of
Alexandria hadn't burned down,
would I know another word for
bluebirds, now?
If I didn't spend so much time thinking
about dead and dusty things,
would I know another word for a
lifetime, now?
Maybe the spirits know another word
for bluebird and that's why they keep
showing up
in the reflection of my bathroom mirror.

III.
There are bones underneath the whole Earth,
and yet we wonder why we are cursed.
We put bones into our cars and we
wonder why we can't breathe.
We put bones under our strip malls and
wonder why people disappear into the trees.
You tell me back in Ohio there was a golf
course built on a Native American burial ground.
I tell you that no one remembers what
our traditional clothes look like now, but
my grandmother.
I was not built for the Age of Extinction.
I was not built for the Age of
Colonization &
Degradation &
Burned out forests &

Dying languages &
Dying people &
Dying bluebirds.

A New Field Guide to People

Ancestor

There, there, look there, see, the indri,
the babakoto, older brother, son, father.
 The females run their tree-top society.

She/he hitch up, a couple staying together
for good or ill, raise roughhousing offspring,
and never on the prowl for another

partner, till death do them part, sleeping
in pairs, spooning in the high canopy,
defecating in unison, speed-leaping

from tree to tree. If only you could see these
highflying sun-worshippers pray,
or listen to their singing, their own *Hiragas*:

the chorus, solos, duets, in accordance with the day,
their songs of songs, crying to their siblings gone astray.

Alone

Sylvia Chapman, 16, Huntington, VT

I'm a person who really does enjoy
being alone, but,
sometimes alone can get lonely.
So I hold my own hand
and picture his hand in mine.

Bacteria

Indefatigable, microbial, impossibly mutable.
Grand words to describe each nano sphere, spiral, rod,
and now add ubiquitous, multitudinous, inestimable,

invisible and you've a sense of them, as close to a god
as we'll ever get. Right now they crawl, float, sprint,
Fosbury Flop, pole vault, lean on their canes, maraud,

crack flabellum whips, plod between lines, the print
you're reading this on; others skinny dip in the water
you drink, all without giving you the merest hint

they are, they exist, weighing heavier all together
than ourselves all together – believe it.
They can be our misfortune and our savior,

our cohorts, both loathsome and exquisite.
If skeptical then take a whiff of your arm pit.

Clouds

Ruth Knox, 12, Essex Junction, VT

I.
 My brain finds every little fluff of
cloud in the sky.
 I think it's because part of me
wants nothing to be forgotten. Neither
the little fluff of white, nor the large,
flat cloud that's laid out like a blanket
across the sky. I enjoy searching for
the small things, looking at the
different shapes in the mulch or
counting the leaves on a flowery
bush. Looking at the overlooked. It's
satisfying, in a way. Looking at the
things that aren't quite considered
beautiful. Like the clouds that cover
the bright stars. They just want a
moment to shine, but instead they
just annoy the watchers.
 Focusing on the things that are
still there, part of this universe,
and doing something — it's such
an odd feeling. I enjoy it, though.
Knowing I'm acknowledging the
overlooked. Knowing that I can see
 that it is there, rather than just turning
away from it because it disappoints me. Strange.
 It's like how sometimes I tell
myself, *That wouldn't happen to me.*
There are so many other people in the

world! I overlook the fact that, well,
they are individuals. They're little fluffs
of cloud in the sky. One person
can be considered insignificant, like
a leaf on a tree, but they are still· there.
   We are all here, whether you look
at us or not.

Caribbean Monk Seal

The Caribbean Sea Wolf, the Monk Seal
was a goner from the get-go: friendly,
docile, curious, innocent, without any real

sense of danger after 'hauling out' of the sea,
basking on a paradisiacal, atoll beach;
prelapsarian, unable to comprehend, foresee

the nature of the Fallen after the Garden's breach.
Sailors sprang from boats with club and muzzle.
Something to hear the seals moan and screech,

witness these sleek beings of muscle and fat bustle,
hustle pups into the blood-red surf's commotion,
their whiskered faces flashing grief, panic, puzzle.

Still the killing went on without compunction.
After all, lamps need oil, men need occupation.

Sweet Mother

Zoe Bernstein, 16, Jericho, VT

Sweet Mother, I cannot weave,
for my heartstrings
have grown as brittle
as the saltwater crust on sand.
Sweet Mother, I cannot sing,
for with her last kiss she
has stolen my vocal cords
and stashed them across the sea.
Sweet Mother, I cannot breathe,
as when she took my breath away.
Like a golden ring lost to the waves.
I shall not get it back.

Ectopistes migratorius.

The winged ones are back: the robin, chickadee,
tufted titmouse, nut-hatch, cardinal, song sparrow,
junco, the woodpecker (both palliated and downy),

the goldfinch in his harlequin-happy yellow,
the red-winged blackbird, the mourning dove.
But the most gregarious of the whole show

is nowhere to be seen, and heavens above,
there were more of these beauties than the rest
of all the others combined. What happened to love

of creatures? We set them ablaze, plugged their nests,
pot-shot them from trains, wagons, horses one by done;
clobbered low flyers, had them declared pests.

This bird of many monikers: Long-tailed Dove, Blue One,
Tourte…is forgotten now by its final name, Passenger Pigeon.

Someone

Whitney Dykstra, 15, Monkton, VT

Beauty will never cease
to exist in this world.
It simply goes into hiding
from time
to time
waiting for a special someone
who cares enough
to come looking.
Someone who is
strong in the ways
most of the world is not.
Kindness. Caring. Love.
Someone who will gently peel back
the branches hollowed by suffering
that mark both death and life
anew.
Someone who will caress
sorrowful life left in nature
with true pain in their heart.
Someone willing to apologize
for the hurt, death, and destruction
the entire human race
is responsible for;
Be that someone.

Formicidae

The ant is "your man", or rather "your woman".
The female population run the show,
a gynocracy — the males manage a short lifespan,

just good for you-know-what, then out they go.
These workers tend the nest and queen:
builders, carpenters, plumbers, metro-

workers, undertakers, inspectors of hygiene.
Too old for their trade, they change livelihood,
become foragers, selfless in their new routine,

sacrificing themselves for the collective good,
out-in-the-open prey, like the ant this instant
on our deck, carting food back to the sisterhood,

equivalent to one of us carrying an elephant.
If effort is *real* victory, the ant is triumphant.

Warrior Women

Maria Beaulieu, 17, Milton, VT

A warrior princess
with golden armor
and an aluminum core
told me to keep my anger.

Let it boil and let it rise
until the steam hits your tongue,
and when they chime how you're too
young,
breathe fire from your soul.

Let your words be the embers
fallen at their feet.
Don't let your tears put out the heat —
watch it burn *slowly*.

Warrior goddess princess queen,
with armor that's both palpable and
strong,
teaches me how my anger is passion
and my directness is professional,
shows me that saying no is not being
disagreeable,
just as crying is not weak or womanly,
but humanly.

These lessons I know to be true,
if they are the only facts that I'll ever
know,

because warrior goddess princess queen
is what I see

in tide pools on sunny days,
and when her gaze meets mine.
Mouth in a straight line — not smiling to
appease the masses —
my own reflection floods the frame.

Orca

Something's off about the name *Killer* Whale.
Or, if not, what then should we call the like of us
and many another killer with or without a tail?

Besides, they are dolphins, inhabitants of Orcus,
the ones who rule, make a mere pool
of the ocean underworld; able to chat, discuss

long distance; assist each other; fool,
frolic for hours; are friendly, close;
adore their mothers; attend school,

learn languages, dialects, echoes;
are various as plankton or octopus;
dressed, as if for the Nobel, in tuxedos

(a white tie-and-tails event); size: extra-large +,
widely acclaimed for their formidable genius.

Some Things Glow

Ruby Hoffman, 12, Essex Junction, VT

Some things glow
under the light
of my LED strips,
fading from purple to orange
to red to yellow.
Some things glow, like my neon mask
and my soccer socks.
Like people. Some people,
it's their moment, and others,
they have to wait a little longer
so they can glow,
authentic to themselves.

Parrot

Feather-brained, you kidding? This one is smarter
than I was at six — though, granted, I was slow
according to Brother Dermot, our headmaster,

raising his bamboo cane, "Boy, you're a holy show".
He parroted on about God, sin, hell and purgatory.
Can't spell "abysmal"? Swish. Stand in the dunce row.

Can a parrot have dyslexia, (a word nobody
knew back then)? We were just laggards, lay-
abouts, wasters, slackers, sloths, plain lazy.

Not so, the parrot; consider Alex's precocious display.
The bird could spell, form proper sentences (went to
Harvard even). Asked what color he was: "I'm gray."

Now we are wiping out his chatty, banerry kind too.
His last words: "Be good. See you tomorrow? Love you."

I Hear

Molly Silvia, 13, Shelburne, VT

I hear the birds
singing in the trees.
I hear the whispers
of a cool winter breeze.
I hear the crunch
of my boots on the snow.
The forest gives life,
now you know.

Homo sapiens

It's a bit rich to rant on about how bad
we are, seldom vice-versa. Fear is fair,
but give us our due: we also care, are glad

to help one another, are quick to share,
mourn over whoever or whatever is gone;
we know grief, sadness, and despair

and still (even with grace) struggle on.
Good in the smallest ways: we hold a door
open for strangers, we say please, pardon,

thank you, and would you like some more?
We live together in flocks, herds, hives. We
communicate like whales from shore

to shore. Smarter than squirrel, crow or chimpanzee.
We're wowman, woeman, wemen, youman. We are we.

The Tree Planter

Annika Gruber, 16, Charlotte, VT

   When my grandpa was in fifth
grade he and his father decided
to plant a red maple tree in their
backyard in Missoula, Montana. My
grandpa said he remembered how
small that tree had been when it first
started growing, "about as thin as a
broomstick…"

   When he was a kid, my grandpa's
family moved around a lot so he
didn't have the time to see that tree
grow up the way that he wanted to
when he was younger. Still, he never
forgot about it.

   Even as the years went by, that
little red maple tree was tied to a
special memory of him and his father
doing something good together, and
that was important. In fact, that
memory stayed so strong in my
grandpa's mind that 50 years later he
decided to go back to his childhood
home and check up on that same
tree. He said that when he saw it
again, he noticed that it still stood
just where he and his father had
planted it, except that now it wasn't
as small and thin as a broomstick,
but tall and beautiful and strong

with branches reaching up toward the sun. To see it there made my grandpa proud.

Since that day in the fifth grade, my grandpa has been on a journey of planting trees at every house he has ever lived in. He made a promise that he would do that for the rest of his life, and so far he hasn't broken it.

When I asked my grandfather what he thought that trees might have taught him about his life, he said without hesitation that they have taught him about resilience.

"Trees can get through just about anything," he told me. "They can grow just about anywhere and then stay there for hundreds of years. Animals can build their homes in them, all kinds of weather can hit them, and yet they still stand tall and strong."

I think that's what resilience really means, and now when I look at trees, I think about my grandpa. I think about all the special trees that he has in his life, and how he planted each one of them just so he could watch them grow.

Ivory-billed Woodpecker

"We are just money-grubbers," said James F. Griswold, Chicago Mill's chairman of the board, during the meeting [regarding logging that would endanger this woodpecker]. "We are not concerned, as are you folks, with ethical considerations."

From Hope is the Thing with Feathers, Christopher Cokinos

Play the drum slowly, the Ivory's drum
rolls no more. We've searched. Facts accrue.
We put a price on its head, a tidy sum.

No sign of that stripe running from neck to
wing, its distinctive perky mien,
its common *cant* call, though it is true

that rumors of sight and sound have been
bruited: that one along the remote bayou
of the Pearl River raised hope, sent keen

birders to glean the truth, but alas, another blow.
Bewail the money-grubbers, the logging spurred
to make gun chests and coffins. Admire Brinkley though,

a town quick to make a killing, scuttlebutting word
of Lord-God-Bird sightings, the good Lord Bill Bird.

The Missing Tree

Max Liebon, 16, Post Mills, VT

A stunted, scraggly tree sat among a few crumpled beer cans and soggy fast food wrappers in a small patch of graying and equally scraggly grass by the side of a highway somewhere in New England. A few dewdrops fell from its branches; forming a small, murky puddle at its base. The dreary November morning allowed little sun through its gray, cloud-laden sky, and what did get through the tree greedily soaked up with the few leaves still hanging on to its thin, gnarled branches. The tree's roots wormed their way through the dusty and far-from nutritious soil, lapping up the minerals they found with vigor, bordering on obsession.

The tree paid little attention to these things. It was busy making a plan. You see, the tree had been there since it was a seed, and had worked hard to earn itself a place among the ill-kempt grass patches·and Bud Light cans, only to be ignored by just about everyone. As you might expect, it was rather fed up with it all. It had long resolved to leave, but hadn't ever quite gotten around to figuring out how to do so. The problem, it thought, was that it was a tree, which, as you might know, is strictly forbidden from moving of its own accord. But it had no intent of letting this stop it.

As the tree thought these things, something happened. This something was not the sort of

something you might expect to be especially
relevant to a tree, but in this case, you would
be wrong. The something was a fight. More
specifically, it was a fight between a man and
his wife. The wife was tired of him drinking all
their money away, and decided to tell him so, in a
manner that involved more screaming and raging
than actual telling. The man, quite tired of being
called worthless about a thousand times, decided
that he needed to visit a nearby bar, to cool off
a little, and to waste all his money, which just so
happened to be one of his favorite pastimes. In
fact, he passed the tree just as it was beginning to
give up pondering how it, as a tree, would move.

A few hours later, the tree had given up entirely,
and the man felt drunk enough to go home. He
stumbled out of the bar, hopped into his truck,
and trundled off. Just as he was passing by the
tree, as he had done hundreds of times on his way
to and from the bar, a gust of wind wafted by;
carrying a few fast food containers with it. These
blew in front of the man, who, as it happens, was
drunk enough that he couldn't tell the difference
between a piece of trash and a small animal, but
just barely not drunk enough that it didn't occur
to him to swerve out of the way. He skidded
across the width of the highway, right over its
edge, and straight into the tree, easily uprooting it
from its place in the rocky soil.

The tree, seeing its chance, promptly got up and
walked away, earning itself a few dark looks from
its grassy neighbors, who took abiding by the laws
of nature more seriously. The man was vaguely

28

aware of the fact that something unusual had happened, but he decided it best to simply drive home and hope no one had noticed.

Luckily for both of them, few noticed the tree was missing, and those who did, mostly assumed it had been removed by a road crew, or some equally unoriginal story. The road crew also noticed it was gone, but had other matters to attend to, albeit ones that were no less mundane than a missing tree.

Japanese River Otter

"If you have a stole, coat, hat, belt,
any garment made of otter fur
it just might be the expensive pelt

of this Japanese beauty", said the furrier.
(Odd to think we wear any creature's skin,
a thought we tend to shun, hide). The spur

to their eventual demise: the Zen
of the yen. And, we *do* need to stay warm.
Lutra lutra whiteleyi won't be seen again.

Done in, to boot, by the spew of harm
we brush under carpets of river and sea.
This playful creature had such charm,

a cure, an emblem last sighted in Susaki,
celebrated in better days by the otter poet, Shiki.

Humans in 6 Words

Katherine Moran, 15, Bristol, VT

I am. We make. It's finished.

King Rail

The king rail, rare to catch sight of as it is,
and getting, we're told, rarer by the day,
and not just because it blends in, is easy to miss:

its lanky body designed to make its stealthy way
between rushes, sedges, reeds; so sleek,
its long claws balancing on silence, splay-

ing outwards, discreet, a downright sneak;
so clever, so expert at going unseen
that little's known about them, a survival technique

that may lead to its ironic demise. On lean
days these pescatarians are known to resort
to dryland bugs — maybe then they can be seen,

or you'll catch one come out in the open to court,
the male waving his surrender flag's white covert.

To the Fig Tree on Koloêp Island

Sam Aikman, 17, Richmond, VT

When I say "fig"
I do not mean the kind
you get at the supermarket
in a clear plastic tub.
I do not mean the kind
that is shriveled, and brown,
and crackles when cleaved open
by a child with dirty nails.
When I say "fig"
l mean the kind that dangles,
purple and glowing,
from a thicket of foliage
above a cobbled street.
Have you ever stood
at the edge of the Adriatic
under the shade of a tree
as old as a country
and eaten the pith of a fruit
the color of the sky at dusk?
What is this sudden urge we call
longing?
When, in the late afternoon
of a Saturday in January
as you loiter under
the fluorescent lights
in aisle six, you demand to
have the heart
of a past summer on your tongue.
You buy a box despite them being old and dry,

and stand with your fingers in your mouth
at a bus stop on the corner of Dorset,
halfway around the world
from the tree
that has not likely been long
lost to sun.
When you consider the heat,
and the distance, and all the time
it takes to deliver life (first to your
palm and then to your lips),
really, what is the point
of waiting a moment longer
before returning
to the fig on Kolocêp Island?
Since when has fruit never been
enough of a reason to leave?

Little Fly

So, Mr. Green, what's good about the mosquito,
Princess Proboscis, Lady Vampire, Ms. Vector,
Dame Disease, *Madam la Mort*: yellow

jack, dengue, encephalitis, this fever, that fever,
The female serial killer beyond compare?
Jab, jab your dead, or you'll never

be the same again, pal. What a flare
for terminating millions. You
scratch that flaming itch. Why should she care?

She is doing what we all want to do:
she just wants to spread, to flourish,
a link in the chain. Exterminate her and we'd rue

the decline of the swallow, bat, duck, the fish
you have for dinner. Be careful of what we wish.

Underestimating

Julia Todd, 14, South Burlington, VT

I forgot the tree in my yard
bloomed so beautifully,
never knew my friends were
so much more
amazing than I thought
(or liked this or were good at that);
failed to understand how
complex people are,
beyond the hours,
the few spoken words
during which our lives overlap.
The world reminds me,
peeling fruit I'd never sliced into
because it was too bruised
for me to accept.
But not all parts are rotten,
and there's strength in the soft spots
that I didn't notice.
The world nudges me
in the shoulder,
trying to turn my eyes
from the mirrors and journals
and *pay attention* for once, because
more things matter than myself,
and I'm blocking those around me
with unnecessary thoughts.
And the world blows lists in my face,
of kindnesses, favors,
thank-you notes, to-do lists (but not

because *I have to do*). But maybe it's
actually important to step back
and be grateful for once,
or twice, or always.
My brain sets bars
and boxes people in,
assuming abilities, labeling lives,
taking too much for granted.
When these people break through,
away from my judgments, I get it.
Starting to understand that
my expectations are as flimsy as
dental floss that
needs to be thrown out.
Starting to try to
let people flow without my mind's
assumptions.
Still, I'm scared.
Even breakable barriers leave marks
in your skin when they snap,
floss wrapped too tightly,
cutting off circulation,
and nobody deserves this from me.

Moa

And these flightless birds were in their element
on their own two legs, could reach 15 feet or more,
tearing and clipping the tastiest, most succulent

leaves without lifting a foot off the floor.
Who needs wings in that sort of paradise?
Their only fear the giant *Poukai* of lore,

itself a creature gone belly-up, paying the price
for relying solely on moa meat. When eventually
another wingless creature arrived --numerous as lice--

and fell upon the moa, no mercy was shown: the Maori,
who themselves would be set upon by their own ilk
and to the present day — but that is another story.

Or is it? Above extinction's wildlife park
the moa's long neck rises like a great ⸮

The Firsts and the Lasts

Roxanne Glassenberg, 17, Burlington, VT

When will the last owl fly
calling-out for why and who?
When will the last Wolf howl
up at a heavy silver moon?
When will the very last salmon
swim upstream to spawn?
When will come the final sparrow?
Crow? Finch? Swan?
It's going to be in my lifetime, I fear,
though I hate to make this about me,
For really it's about the birds and
trees and fish in the rising sea.
It's about the lists we make,
calling them "endangered."
When, of course, it's our own fault,
and we were too slow to anger.
The human mind loves to categorize,
even as we drive them and us extinct.
We won't be the last, but we sure are the first,
on our planet, to think and not think.

Northern Bog Lemming

These poor rodents, cute fairy-tale rats,
are the victims of so much baloney.
What people believe is often bats:

Zieglar of Stalwart, circa 1530,
spread the notion that the lemmings hailed
out of the heavens during stormy

weather, and, beat this, that they all ailed
and died with the very first spring sprigs.
Or, how about the cliché that's prevailed?

When this rodent, who shits emerald droppings
moves *en masse*, it is for lack of habitat.
At this point the Northern bog lemmings

have been driven over the edge — the changing climate
their cliff — more manslaughter than suicide at any rate.

My Eyes

Scarlett Cannizzaro, 13, Essex, VT

For so long,
I have listened to others –
others' opinions
others' words.
I have heard them speak,
I have heard them debate,
and I have only
wished a single thing:
to be able to know
what I agree with.
In this world,
I am realizing that
there are many, many struggles —
there are things that so many
people feel strongly about —
and I am finding that
I truly don't know
how I feel about these topics.
What is my opinion?·
For a while,
I would listen to those I
know closely,
and I would nod
as they talked about
their thoughts on something.
1 would immediately think,
This must be the right decision if
it's coming from them.
However,

if there is anything I've learned
from experiencing this pandemic,
it is that not everyone agrees. Not
everyone agrees,
even if they are friends,
even if they are family;
and that is alright.
I no longer feel like my opinion
has to depend
on the opinions of those
I trust,
those I have gotten to know.
I want to find my own opinions,
I want to have my own strong feelings,
and I want to know how to share them in
the right way,
in a respectful way,
in a civilized way.
I want to look at the world from my eyes
not from others,
but mine.

Interlude

Psalm 23, A Secular Take

The earth is our shepherd, we should not want.
She restoreth our spirits. She leadeth us
      in the ways of righteousness for all our sakes.
Yea, as we walk through the valley of the shadow
      of life we should fear evil. But She is with us.
Her flora and fauna nurture us.
She prepareth a table before us in the presence
          of our friends.
She grants us the fruits of our toil;
Our cup runneth over.
Surely goodness and mercy will follow us
      all the days of our dying
and we shall dwell in the bounty of our Mother. Awemen.

Mine Garden

Zoe Bernstein, 16, Jericho, VT

Thy woods be not for conquering
but for running swift and long.
From wolf,
toward deer.
With river,
on Earth.·
Ye ivy be not for pruning,
but unfurling and undoing.
His forest be not for lumber,
but be sweet, low song
of oak trees.
Mine garden be not
for nurturement of my own,
but of all the rabbits and bees.

Fuse

After the haunting quiet of two minutes' silence for the planet we heard it, a rumble, something alive, a people wave rolling over thousands along the Avenue.

From an online report after the Climate March, NY, Sep 21ˢᵗ2014

The demon-
stration
stretches far
as the eye can-
not see, down
Central Park
West, be-
tween the green
world and the high-
rise bluffs.
The inflated
plastic planet
is kept afloat
batted from hand to
hand: Gaia.
Mammon trawls
her into his net.
Two minutes' silence,
then a wave
of cheers, alarms,
raised arms charges
towards us.
It's like someone
lit a human fuse
sizzling alight,
detonating spirit-
dynamite.

Smoke

Ava Rohrbaugh, 15, Charlotte, VT

Children born in smoke
let it circle their cradles.
They fill their cheeks with
cold hunks of coal and
let the embers
warm their toes.
Children born in smoke
can breathe much easier
when the burning ends,
since they learned to
live in the chimney
stack before they could count.
Children born in smoke
know how to light a fire.

Postdated Earth Day Poem, 2035, Give or Take

(To many Politicians and the Corporate World especially)

Finally, no-holds-barred legislation is brought out.
Even erstwhile oil and gas lobbyists work for wind
and solar, righteously demand that no one must flout

"our only home". Politicians and corporations contend,
boast even, that it is they who bring change about,
("Reknew by Renewables or We All Shall End

up Fossils", the latest slogans). In a way they're right:
it's they more than any — though really most everyone
in one way or many played our part — turned day to night,

conjuring storms, the poles coming undone,
record mercury readings, fires, floods, drought,
cities wiped out, crops failing, shrouding of the sun,

contagious fogs, frogs and bees dying, the death
of millions. More than others we owe them this debt.

The Politician Became a Painter

Alex Escaja-Heiss, 15, South Burlington, VT

Blue eyes roam shelves lined with mass-
produced white acrylic paint,
trying to find the best shade for the best
quantity for the best value for the best
unit price.
He chooses a container, perfectly sealed,
no sharp comers or plastic that he could
(accidentally)
cut his hand on.
He paints a face,
a square face
with blue eyes.
He paints stubble.
He does not emphasize the lips.
He does not want the painting to look
feminine.
He does not emphasize the lashes.
He does not want the painting to look
gay.
He does not shade.
He does not want the painting to look
black.
He does not want the painting to look
real.
The painting is displayed in a museum.
Hundreds attend his funeral.

At the Yeats International Summer School

"You're being hysterical", a poet accuses,
"a bit like those women of 'Lapis Lazuli'".
Under such strain you abuse the muses."

He scoffs, turns away with a sigh,
mounts the lofty slope, takes a break
under a wayside tree, peers from on high,

lilts a melody, sips laced tea, nibbles his cake,
demurs on all the tragic scene below.
He picks the strings of art for art's sake.

Other players join in, a deafening holy show.
It's all a cycle, so why fret, cause a sensation?
We ride in on ass-horse-camel-tank-back and we go.

No need here for further word indignation.
He strums the air-guitar of his tergiversation.

Last Words from Human to Pale Bear

Astrid Longstreth, 13, West Bolton, VT

I see you, Pale Bear,
posing atop a glacier
that is sinking,
your white fur glistening in the pale
sunlight of the Arctic,
eyes seeing, looking, searching
for a way to escape.

I see you, Pale Bear,
perched precariously on an iceberg that
is shrinking,
icy waves lapping at your feet.

I see you, Pale Bear,
and I want to wave to you, but I don't
know if you will have the time to reply.

I see you, Pale Bear,
and I want to say goodbye -
for I'm not sure how much longer you'll
last before descending into the deep.

I see you, Pale Bear,
and want to say my last words to you -
though I'm not quite sure what to say.

I see you, Pale Bear,
and whisper words unheard beneath
the gusting wind.

Pale Bear, oh, Pale Bear ... I'm sorry for all
we have done. And, Pale Bear, I'll try -
oh I'll try, to rescue you from the ocean
that is ever rising
higher
        higher
                higher.
But, Pale Bear, I fear I am too late.
So, Pale Bear, all that is left to say is for
you to dig your claws in deeper, hold on
a little longer, and we'll try to do the
rest. For we are the problem, Pale Bear,
and you have simply been caught up in
our reign of terror.

I see you, Pale Bear ...
I see you.

"Bar Bar"

"Let me say it openly: we are surrounded by an enterprise of degrada-
tion, cruelty, and killing which rivals anything that the Third Reich was
capable of, indeed dwarfs it, in that ours is an enterprise without end,
self-regenerating, bringing rabbits, rats, poultry, livestock ceaselessly into
the world for the purpose of killing them."

J.M. Coetzee, from The Lives of the Animals

The lecturer quotes Adorno, "Writing poetry
after Auschwitz is barbaric."
Barbarous to compare this atrocity

with that, reduce each to the generic,
but consider, say, what many of us wear,
what most daily eat and drink, our trick

of general tergiverse everywhere.
How was your beef, salmon, veal?
Have you ever visited a farm anywhere?

Surely pigs can't really think or feel?
Then there's testing mice, monkey and chick
for the sake of curing a child. A lousy deal

for creatures. Excuse me waxing didactic.
If this is poetry then it's nothing bar barbaric.

No Bows

Callyx O'Donnell, 15, Hinesburg, VT

I want to pull the ribbon
of my emotions,
my thoughts and feelings,
out through my mouth,
and tie it
in a beautiful bow.
But each time I reach
into that well between my chin
and collarbone,
all I pull out is a tangled string
that is unruly and thin.
It's the kind of string
you can't tie bows with,
and I am infuriated that my tongue
stumbles
over the knotted syllables
and fumbles blindly
with the mangled social skills.
I wish
to tie a bow with the words
that I want to flow
from my mouth,
but all I have is a heap
of intertwined threads
that lie at my feet,
mocking me instead.

The Noble Lie

I am a citizen of the country where truth
lies. Even now you shouldn't believe me.
I lie my individual, private white lies,
concocted excuses for being late,
harmless fibs to evade a row. Why
make anyone cry? I lie my public lies,
a citizen voting for lesser evils,
a taxpayer dropping the exploding lies
of democracy on unseen people.
The condoned lies of the public
become noble. A lie shared is
a lie made truth, easier to excuse
the black lie, grey lie, blue lie, green lie,
purple lie, yellow lie, the blood-red lie.

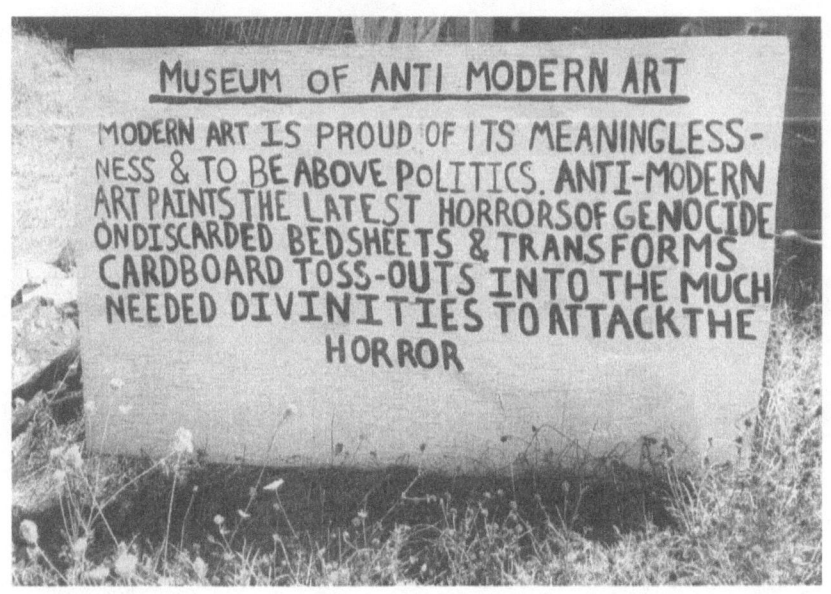

Photo by Greg Delanty

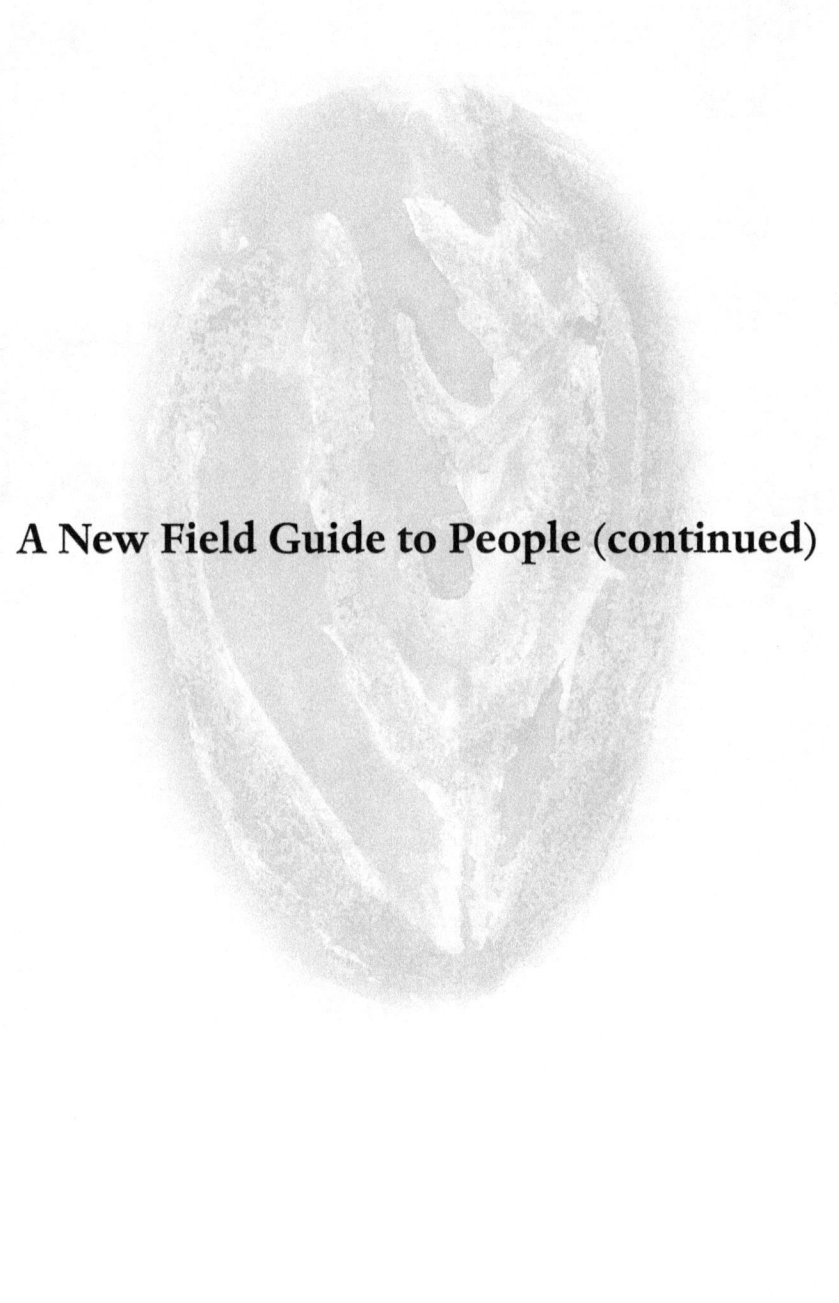

A New Field Guide to People (continued)

Quiver Tree

It is all happening internet fast.
Take the giant quiver tree, the kokerboom, It should
manage — delt with change in the past,

why not now? What with its soaring, wood-
like trunk, sun-screened branches; an aloe.
Community center for the neighborhood.

Fleshy stems reach up, short on H2O,
like hands begging relief from their desert plight,
a *purgatorio* metamorphosed into an *inferno*,

or like the comic-strip hair of characters in fright.
Looks like they see the future, know they'll never
adapt quick enough, can't up and locate to a friendlier site.

From the plant's bark the San people carve arrow quiver.
Fitting that its name is a synonym for *tremble* and *shiver*.

Hidden by the Rain

Emmeline Brewer, 12, Williston, VT

Rain pattered down on her window. Every drop hit the window with its own tone. Its own story. She peered out, watching. There was a single tree, its leaves bright and green against the gray sky. This tree stood tall. Its leaves fluttered and whipped in the wind and rain, but no matter what hit them, they stayed attached. They were strong. Her gaze shifted. Her eyes gazed across the field, long, beige, and soaking wet. They flew over the pond, the cows, and the stable, a red mass against the coming darkness. But no matter where they went, they always came back to that one tree. For some reason, it was captivating. The leaves weren't perfect. They had holes from bugs, some were weather-worn, and each was a different color. But that was how it was.

She squinted now, as the rain dumped its last bucket of water. It hammered over her roof, beat down on the stables, and lashed out at the tree, but somehow, somehow it kept its poise. It stood there. As the clouds fell away, wisp by wisp; she ran out. The night was as still as any other. Her bare feet thudded against the ground. Her T-shirt whipped against her side. But she ran. She jumped into that tree. She launched herself into the leaves, the holey, wet, worn, colorful leaves. She had never seen anything as magnificent in her life.

Zea Mays

Amazing. Ah shucks, man. Corny.
They are a swaying sea, a green ocean
stretching across the infinity

of America, setting so much in motion,
a kernel of life, a daily nitty gritty:
your breakfast (with goat's milk), lotion,

tobacco, pipes, tacos; a must at a movie;
heat, automobile fuel, plastic, a power plant,
bread, polenta, chowder, fish bait, hominy.

And being oblivious of shame, innocent,
they know nothing of the human scorn
of the body, of being improper, indecent:

an example of natural and artificial selection,
each expose a green-sheathed erection.

Born from the Mountains

Abhi Dodgson, 12, South Hero, VT

Born from the monsoon rain that falls
like a wall of water onto the dirty streets
washing the roadsides, cleansing them
until they look brand new
I am from the juice of coconuts
that tastes so sweet
I am from the lily pads that float on the
water
I am from spices and flavors that fill this
land with their magnificent smells
I am from the hot sweet-tasting tea
I am from the dark brown earth in the
tea leaf beds
I am from the highest mountains
where the oxygen is thin and harder to
breathe

Rorqual

Largest and loudest creature that ever was or is:
The Blue, Old Sulphur-bottom, Musculus,
Sibbald's Rorqual; with a heart (and penis)

as big as a minibus or ambulance;
guiding one another in ocean-to-ocean song,
communicating through depth and distance.

Our ships, submarines, solar gong,
our black noise drowns them out,
confounds them. They may not have long.

And that's before we spout anything about
mammoth icebergs melting, the sick spume
and the oil and blubber hunter's rout.

Wash your hands. Take that cruise. Spray that perfume.
Ignore the stock crash of climate, the population boom.

Untitled

Anna Phelps, 15, Wolcott, VT

I can't morph into a cloud
if I'm just a rock
just like I can't dream
if I don't have a destiny.

Lonesome George

On June 24, 2012, this tortoise was found dead by Fausto Llerana, his
care-keeper 40 years.

Only his custodian, his keeper, Fausto,
should be on first name terms with this sage,
the last Pinta Island tortoise to go,

a centenarian, which is hearty middle age
for a tortoise. Each day he'd welcome his care:
this humpback speed-creeping from his cage,

He'd stretch his periscopic neck, throat-smell the air,
open his denture-less mouth as if to say, "Hello,
how's it going, Fausto, old boy? Hard for me to bare

the angsts, creeps, slobs of humans at my daily show.
Lonesome is right; all the rest of my own sent ahead
to Tortoise Tartarus, animal Avernus. You know

I know that you feel for us, but when all is unsaid
we live only here now, the Galapagos of the Dead."

Temporarily Forever

Mia Marino, 16, Hinesburg, VT

Though I'm only 16,
I feel 60.
I feel as if I've been through wars.
I feel as if I slept through
the Depression,
only to wake to find
that I'm the president.
I feel as though it were only last
Thursday that I sailed to America
with my great-grandmother.
I feel as if I were once stationed
in the Galapagos Islands
in awe of the animals around me.
I feel as though
I've watched the world come
and go.
I feel as though I am endless.
It's so tiring,
but nobody knows.

Decomposers

Without the recyclers we are nowhere.
Among them the fortitudinous fungi,
a kingdom, or rather empire, everywhere,

though its denizens work mostly
unseen, on the graveyard shift, renew
rotten flesh, resurrect the ghostly

dead. Others are delicious in soup or stew,
just as tasty in burger, sandwich or salad,
give a lift to bread and biscuits, help us brew

excellent beer, and even cure the sick. They add
and add. Time to raise a paean, a chorus
to honor them, even if some drive you mad:

the sneezing-bogey lodged in a sinus,
the foot-itch imp, or yeast's chastity incubus.

Slow Days

Willa Pelschoen, 15, Bolton, VT

When the world is so entirely slow
and beautiful, it rains.
And I walk for ages, picking flowers
and ferns, choosing to forget
all that must be done when I return.

Tea

Early morning, countless folks everywhere,
— it could be anywhere any time of any day —
are having a pot, a cuppa, as I am here;

Barry's Gold, a Cork blend all the way
from the hills of Rwanda, Kenya, India: Assam tea,
Camellia sinensis, cha, chai, tay.

Let me brew a fresh drop for you. You probably
know the drill: scald the pot, measure teaspoon
by teaspoon of leaves, add water — must be

on the boil — allow to steep, pour as soon
as it settles, add milk, sugar, honey, brandy
whatever your fancy, and you're good till noon.

And this Barry's blend is only one of the many,
each with its "agony of leaves", its "tea ceremony".

Early Mornings

Lily Meyer, 12, Montpelier, VT

The sunrise above.
Pink clouds, the smell of coffee.
You watch the sky change.

Ursus arctos crowtheri.

Imagine a tree is found somewhere
in the Atlas Mountains with a kind of ogham,
a script, a scratched story of this bear

clawed into the bark that translates to "I am
last of my kind. But for you we'd still be here.
You stand and sit like us, talk ad nauseam

of how you value the wild, how you care
for all. You who starved, hunted, trapped
us in chains and cages with such flair,

had us fight gladiators, slaves. You were rapt
in forum and circus. The tinnitus of your clap,
cheers and hissing still rings in our ears. It is apt

you have stepped into your own unbearable trap:
the sharp-toothed jaws of the weather snap."

Why Not?

Ashleigh Provost, 17, Hinesburg, VT

Call me a tree hugger,
a hippie, a snowflake.
Tell me I'm exaggerating,
that "trees can't feel."
See my sorrowful gaze
fall across open fields once graced
with exponential growth,
replaced with solid, cold tarmac.
Ask me why I care, why it matters,
I'd admit, I have no convenient
scientific answer.
Is that the only thing
that would settle your discontent?
Have you ever felt the embrace
of a tree? Ever felt the despair
from the life with no voice?
I'll ask you, why don't you care?
As if you do not rest upon
Mother Earth's creation,
as if you do not breathe
the air from her children.
You may ask me
what I gain from caring.
What do you gain by not?

Virus

Get it together, this one can be a terror,
more dreadful than any Nero or Heliogabalus,
invading the body politic cell after cell, mirror

after mirroring into infinity, Emperor Virus
himself or selves. Best treat him well
even as you wash your hands of him. Fuss

over his greatness, tell him he's incomparable.
He's invincible in the armor of his microbe,
usurping the state, taking over every cell.

It would be wise to play the xenophobe
for he is cunning, can outmaneuver, outwit
any defense, wreck havoc across the globe.

And even if it seems that you have him beat,
he'll alter tactics on the double and repeat, repeat.

Perfect for Me

Scarlett Cannizzaro, 13, Essex, VT

When someone says
"perfect"
many immediately think
"flawless".
They hear the word
and they picture no
problems, no issues,
nothing to worry about.
But how perfect
would this world truly be
if there were nothing to
worry about,
nothing to strive for?
If I am scared,
nervous about something,
it simply feels so much better
when I work hard
to acknowledge it,
to achieve it,
to adapt to it, even.
What would life look like
with no goals, no dreams,
nothing to try for?
When someone says
"nothing's perfect",
know that nothing can be
exactly right,
but it can be exactly right for you.
When I think of perfect,

I think of something being
perfect for me,
for my life, for my world.

X

A xonnet for the unknown number of unknown ex
flora and fauna we've crossed out: the x-ikso,
x tree, xanthone flower, Xanthippe dove, the x-

wingéd ones who now we shall never know,
the crucifix rose, the X cuckoo wrasse, the xerox-
butterfly, xylophagous ant, the Aceldama xoco,

the xylophone songbird, the Xanadu ox,
the xenon flower, the xerophilous tree,
the Xanthippe honeybee, the xebec fox,

the ten-spotted ladybird, Xeric bumblebee,
the xylem singer bug, the kiss-kiss carex,
the x cure root, the x signature tree, the ibex flea,

the begonia desert rex, the dolphin haruspex:
the multiplication of ex x ex comes to planet X.

Long Live the Queen

Amica Lansigan, 15, Hanover, NH

We steal her land, exploit her wealth,
and claim it as our own.
We build cities, we sever trees,
destroying our own home.

We do nothing to rebuild
the ruin we create.
We do nothing but watch
as she cries, she burns, and breaks.

We lie to faces, wipe out races,
deny these lies and genocide.
The truth cannot be silenced.
We divide, we war, we side.

Ourselves will be the death of us,
burned in a fire we made.
There will not be a second ark.
This time we can't be saved.

Not one creature will mourn us,
not one tree, ant or swan.
They'll find freedom and happiness
In a world with humans gone.

We thought we were the kings.
But oh, we were such fools.
It was never our kingdom.
The Queen of Nature rules.

The Great Oxygen Event

The one multi-monikered: the Oxygen Holocaust,
the Oxygen Catastrophe, the Great Oxygen
Event, Oxygen Revolution, is the unacknowledged first

extinction — the anaerobic poisoning. So, we're in
the midst of the seventh. What's one more; O tolerant
or no? The credits scroll down too fast to read. Fin.

Most were done in by the oxygen tipping point.
Wham go millions of years and here
we are, the aerobics, the pinnacle of this joint,

Post-Planet Snowball. What would be there
if they had survived and we are not.
(Take a deep breath: ah, that bracing air.)

Maybe they'd have made a more superior lot.
Anything is possible. We too are a long shot.

The River Speaks

Ursa Goldenrose, 13, Hardwick, VT

There is a web
and it holds us.
Pieces come apart,
so we help rebuild it.
We are a species
that has forgotten
our place
on the web,
so the earth reminds us.
It shows us that
there are some lines
that we do not cross,
and if we do cross them,
the water rises,
pushing us back.
The water comes
and it takes.
It's the destruction of what we've built,
but also
the reconstruction
of the natural world.
The water roars,
it cries,
and it heals,
even when we feel hurt.
It washes over land
that was stolen
and poisoned.
It warns us

as we build our walls.
The river speaks.
It wills us to understand years of neglect,
hurt, and carelessness
that have seeped into the sand.
The river is strong,
stronger than us.
It will
reclaim its path,
slowly healing the world.
We are a thread
in a web that
is breaking.
We have forgotten
the path.
We have forgotten
the way
the river speaks.
It wills us to understand —
this is not just our land.

Western Black Rhino

Mister Cataclysmo, Master Hysterical, Squire Adieu,
Sir Gregorian Cant of this divine horror show,
we are better suited to record the inferno than to

praise, praise being the harder word-way to go,
to tune your strings to the harmony, including all
we've managed since the Great Rift yonks ago.

We spread to every corner on our crooked ball.
But right now take a look at this newspaper photo:
a decapitated head leaning against a custom's wall.

The last of its kind, the Western Black Rhino,
the ivory horn ready to be hacksawed off to the meat.
We've brought the rhino down for the sake of a placebo,

a cure-all procured by the distant, well-oiled elite.
The head is like a Halloween mask. Trick or treat?

The Burden of Righteous Fury

Yejun Park, 15, Tallahassee, FL

Most of the time I find myself angry
and it's the kind of anger that you
hold onto, you know, fists tight
stomach burning, because someone has
to be
angry. No one else is angry.
Isn't that unfair?
Isn't that wrong?

And the anger is heavy
and the anger hurts
and this anger was meant for a world
that is not angry when it should be
and it is too much for me,
but who else will be angry?

Yangtze Dolphin

This peace symbol, flagbearer of all left behind, is gone.
Ditto the blue antelope, string tree, Society Parakeet,
Sri Lanka legume, Scioto madtom, Barbary lion.

And these are just the recognized, named elite.
So many unknown others should be on the list.
Time to human-up, nix the I can't do anything bullshit.

The old gods of the weather are mightily pissed.
We're all in the same boat, but Noah is where?
There are too many of us. Our craft lists.

Batten down the hatches. The hull needs repair.
No other way of saying this, the future looks stark.
And most of us carry on with nary a care.

A shroud of cloud drops in dusk-becoming-dark.
Summon in the living. The planet is our only ark.

Saran Wrap

Liza Duchesneau, 14, Milton, VT

I am Saran Wrap
I wrinkle and contort and frustrate
I stick to whatever is nearby
And when there is nothing
I stick to myself
I suffocate
I wrap myself around the fresh necks
The surrendered leftovers
They can't escape me
Dewy moisture dangles from my insides
The perspiration, condensation, sensation
    of longing
My preserves condensing under the
    tightly stretched plastic
They can see right through me
A lucid vision through one dimension
The simplicity of my purpose
Underestimated
I sit in the drawer
I am a shadow
A roll of predictability
For the first sheet matches the second
Matches the third
My matter is identical
My identity doesn't matter.
I coil around a hollow tube
Shriveling
Constricting
Suffocation to the rhythm of temperature

As warm fingers rip me from my
    dimness
Dragging me along jagged teeth
Until I break
Tear
Hoping I will fit their needs
Pulling me tighter and tighter
Stretching me until suffocation is the
    only power I possess all my own
They can see right through me
I am fake
I am plastic
They ball me up
They throw me in the trash
They use me until I'm useless
Until my insides are rotten
I am Saran Wrap

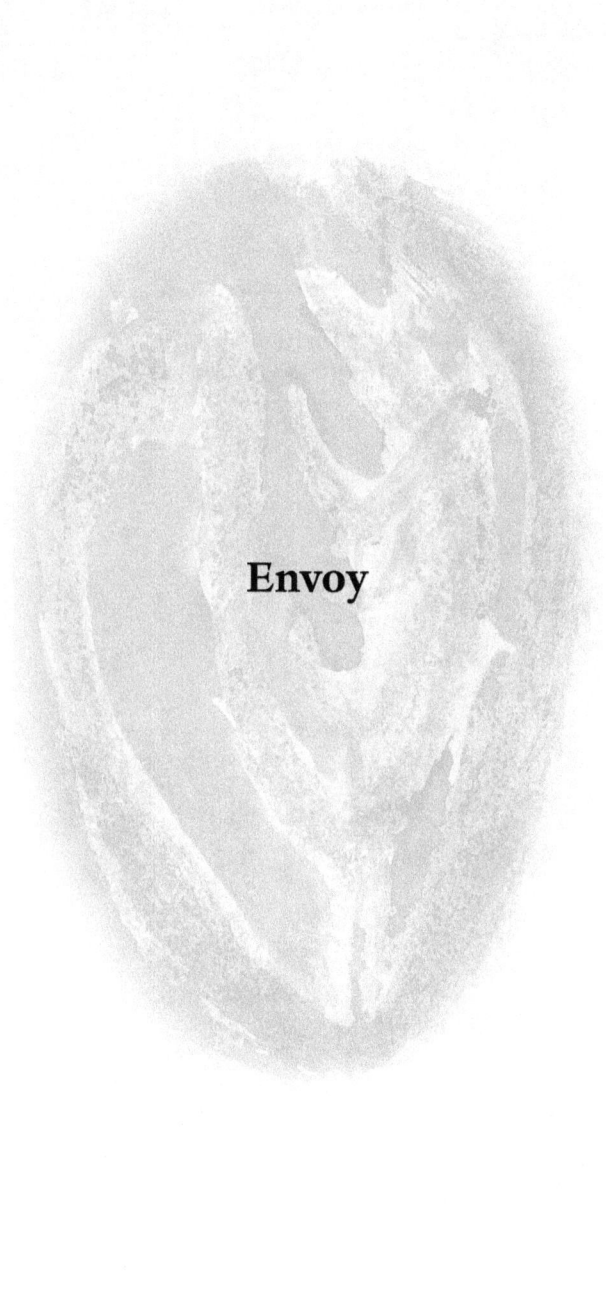

Envoy

Ur Garden

A pear's tricky. Hard to judge
        just by squeezing. Wait
till it's begun to rot, a few days,
        no more. So juicy you better
eat it while no one's around.
        Hold it by the nipple,
        that fulsome breast.

If the apple was the earthly fruit
        not to be touched in the Garden,
the pear is the unearthly one
        that the Maker — having picked up
a snaky trick or two — tempts us
        to taste and we will
        know again the garden.

Daisies, Daffodils, and Dandelions

Evey Slavik, 14, Burlington, VT

Proof of Mother Earth's power,
sprouting from the ground,
reaching for the sky.
Holding their poise as the
wind blows and they dance,
swaying with the breeze,
roots binding them to the earth.
They're like sunshine in a garden,
the closest thing to perfect.
Their large petals placed,
creating a star.
Others with little petals arranged,
still forming a beautiful flower,
with creamy yellows next to
a bold white and shades of green
Hinting at fresh beginnings.

The Jar of Effulgence

Driving in brumal, bucolic Vermont, I take a wrong
      turn, preoccupied with the radio news:
climate change, war, famine, the whole ding-dong;
      how we must choose
          as the fumes in the rear-view mirror are lowlit
          by the cold, contributing our own little bit.

The snow glistens, calling to mind the jar
of effulgence shattering not just over
          this snowland, but over
      the chrome of a passing car,
      the farmyard's heap of manure,
even the silk-lined jackets
      of the prating Suits
      stalking the hallways
      of the Night House, hoarding the shards of light
      in underground shelters out of sight,
lying now through the din of the airways.

Now relax,
we must not let their dark
shroud our lightning-bug existence,
rob us of our modicum of pax,
our birthright spark,
the litscape heliographing,
the light within responding.

I locate myself again, spotting
      Camel's Hump slouching
      through this white country.

The seeds, shards, sparks of effulgence
shimmer over all and sundry.

Peace and Rage

Janet McIntosh, 18, East Shoreham, VT

Peace.
There are pieces of peace scattered across
the hills,
thrown in corners with abandoned
spider webs
and forgotten for decades.
Those pieces of peace do not deteriorate.
They only wait
patiently.
Observant eyes and carefully attuned
ears can pick them out,
track them down,
gently pick them up
and blow the cobwebs away,
returning happiness, laughter,
sunlight trees,
companions to the world.
Peace reincarnated piece by piece.
Rage is red like a ruby.
It burns through everything in its way,
trailing hot coals and lifeless ashes in its
wake.

Rage.
These four letters are weighed down by
so much emotion.
Clenched fists / gritted teeth / furrowed
brows / tight face.
Rage bubbles up inside me

like water boiling over the edges of the
pot,
spilling and leaping from it rim, to fizz,
hiss and spit
on the burner below.
Spit.
Hiss.
Spit.

From Woody's Restaurant, Middlebury

Today, noon, a young macho friendly waiter and three diners,
      business types — two males, one female —
are in a quandary about the name of the duck paddling
      Otter Creek,
the duck being brown, but too large to be a female mallard.
      They really
want to know, and I'm the human-watcher behind the nook
      of my table,
camouflaged by my stillness and nonchalant plumage.
      They really want to know.
This sighting I record in the back of my *Field Guide to People*.

Notes

Ancestors: In Madagascar folktales establish a close relationship between this lemur and humans, and a common ancestry. Two brothers were believed to have lived together in the forest until one of them decided to leave and cultivate the land. That brother became the first human, and the brother who stayed became the first indri. The indri cries in mourning for his brother who went astray. *Hiragasy* is a musical tradition, a day-long spectacle of music, dance, and kabary oratory.

"Bar Bar": The *Greeks* used the term *barbarian* for all non-Greek-speakers. This was because the languages they spoke sounded to Greeks like "bar...bar..;".

Parrot: Alex is the name of an African Grey Parrot. Alex was an acronym for "avian language experiment", or "avian learning experiment". At two years of age he was correctly answering questions made for six-year-old children. Alex was said to have understood the syntax used in language. He called an apple a "banerry" (pronounced as rhyming with some pronunciations of "canary"), which a linguist thought to be a combination of "banana" and "cherry", two fruits he was more familiar with.

The Noble Lie: The concept of a noble lie is a myth or a lie in a society that either emerges on its own or is propagated by an elite in order to maintain social order for the "greater good".

The Museum of Anti-Modern Art: The Museum of Anti-Modern Art is part of the Bread & Puppet Theater.

Lonesome George: All names for a group of tortoises: *angt, creeps, slobs*

Tea: The phrase "agony of leaves" is used by the tea trade which means the unfolding or unfurling of tea leaves in hot water.
Ritual tea drinking, which originated in China, was first practiced in Japan during the Kamakura period (1192-1333 by Zen monks. The tea ceremony has many purposes. It means different things to different people. For some, it is a deeply spiritual practice, all about the meditation and relaxation. For others it is all about the social gathering.

About the Author

Greg Delanty is the author and editor of more than twenty poetry books. He teaches at Saint Michael's Collage, Vermont. He has received many awards, including a Guggenheim for poetry. In 2021 he was awarded The David Ferry & Ellen LaForge Poetry Prize. He is considered both a US/Vermont poet as well as an Irish poet. His work is frequently anthologized and broadcast. Recently one of his poems, "The Alien", featured in Wes Anderson's movie, *Asteroid City*. He has poems forthcoming in numerous venues, including *The Irish Times* and *The Best American Poetry 2025*. For further information see his website: www.gregdelanty.com

"Greg Delanty's work addresses events as varied as the fallout from Chernobyl and the Iraq wars. Most of all, he has become a leading voice on environmental issues. Delanty has spent years tackling the social and political turmoil of our time. Readers see him bring the human destruction of the natural world into his poetic awareness, as early as in poems like "An Oil Spillage," which appears in 1992's *Southward*. The poem ends with the ominous line, "None can escape the dark spreading here." In contemporary poetry, Delanty's voice is not only one that is always engaging with poetic tradition and renewal but also one that is forward-looking and aware of the social, environmental, and political moment."
— from "Out of the Ordinary: The Poetry of Greg Delanty," by Daniel Johnson in *New Hibernia Review*

About Young Writers Project

The young writers' work appears courtesy of Young Writers Project (YWP). The writing was selected from several volumes of YWP's annual anthology, and the ages listed reflect the age of the writer when the work was first published. Many thanks to YWP executive director Susan Reid (2018-current) for her assistance with this book.

YWP is a creative, online community of teens that started in Burlington, Vermont in 2006 with a mission to inspire, mentor, publish, and promote young writers and artists.

To learn more about YWP, to see the work of young writers and artists, or to donate to support YWP's work, visit their website, https://youngwritersproject.org/. Donations are tax deductible and allow YWP to provide all programs free of charge.